KYOGEN

photographs by Tatsuo Yoshikoshi

written by Hisashi Hata

translated and edited by Don Kenny

HOIKUSHA
保育社

Author's Preface

Humor has been very much a part of the arts and literature of Japan throughout the centuries, all the way from the *haiku* verses of the ancient 'Manyoshu' (Japan's oldest collection of poetry, written by emperors and aristocrats between 300 and 750 a.d.) to *rakugo* (mimed storytelling which originated during the early Edo Period, in the 17th century). Kyogen is a comic theatre form that has been passed down on the stages of Japan for the past six hundred years. But Kyogen does not simply provoke laughter. It is also a spontaneous reflection of the customs, the lifestyle, and the morals of the commoners of the middle ages. Since the dialogue of Kyogen is in the language of the 15th and 16th centuries, its scripts are valuable linguistic material for research into the development of the Japanese language. Also in recent years, Noh and Kyogen have made an important contribution to modern theatre due to their simple dramaturgy and powerful acting techniques, aspects which make them seem the freshest and newest of all theatre forms when performed by truly fine actors.

Recently the number of people who enjoy Kyogen has increased greatly. There are numerous Kyogen fans among the very young. Even so, it cannot be said that the general public is truly familiar with the art. Of course, this is due in part to the lack of opportunity to see Kyogen easily and often, resulting in many people attending a single performance under adverse conditions, which makes them lose interest in becoming more familiar with Kyogen. But there are many, many more who have categorically decided that they have no interest in it without having ever come into direct contact with it at all, aside from the two or three scripts they were forced to read during their early school days.

This book has been written for those people who have never seen Kyogen or who have just begun to see and enjoy it. A certain amount of technical information has been included, but generally, the attempt has been made to present practical information that will aid in the enjoyment of actual performances.

Contents

Front Cover — Sensaku Shigeyama in the title role of 'The
God of Happiness' *(Fuku no Kami)*

Kataginu — a shoulder-piece

K Y O G E N

by Tatsuo Yoshikoshi & Hisashi Hata
translated and edited by Don Kenny

© All rights reserved. No.39 of Hoikusha's Color Books
Series.Published by Hoikusha Publishing Co., Ltd., 8-6,
4-chome, Tsurumi, Tsurumi-ku, Osaka,538 Japan. ISBN
4-586-54039-7. First Edition in 1982. 2nd Edition in 1991.
Printed in JAPAN

1. Manzo Nomura as the Shinto Priest in 'The Rice Planting Ceremony' (Ta-ue)

Kyogen History

The Name 'Kyogen'

We will begin our discussion with an explanation of the origin of the name by which this art of comic theatre is known. In the not too distant past, human-interest page newspaper headlines often carried such terms as 'kyogen robbery' or 'kyogen suicide.' Used in this manner, the word means 'frame-up,' 'shame,' or 'fake.' This may seem an overly rambunctious way in which to begin a discussion of a classical theatre art, but the point is that the word *kyôgen* is used in Japanese in a very broad sense to mean 'play,' 'drama,' 'theatre piece,' or, if you will, 'fake performance.'

1

2. Mannojo Nomura as the Monkey Groom (dancing) and Manzo Nomura as the Monkey Father-in-law (sitting far right) in 'The Monkey Groom (Saru Muko)

The Chinese characters used today for the word appear in Japanese literature as early as the ancient collection of poems known as the 'Manyoshu' (see Author's Preface). It was introduced here from the Chinese Classics, where it was read *tawakoto* and meant 'nonsense' or 'crazed irresponsible utterances.' It seems that the reading *kyôgen* came into general use in the term *kyôgen kigo*, which first appeared in the works of the Chinese poet Po Chu-i (772-846 a.d.) included in the 'Japanese and Chinese Poetry Collection' (*Wakan Rôei Shû*; compiled in 1013 a.d.). There are many delicate and complicated nuances of meaning in *kyôgen kigo*. It was originally a Buddhist term that meant 'fancy words that draw people away from the correct teachings of the true way of Buddha.' Thus is came to mean 'fabrication' or 'fiction.'

3. Mannosuke Nomura as the Fox and Mansaku Nomura as the Trapper in the second part of 'Fox Trapping' (Tsuri-Gitsune)

4. Mannosuke Nomura as the Fox (disguised as the Trapper's Uncle Hakuzosu) and Mansaku Nomura as the Trapper in the first part of 'Fox Trapping' (Tsuri-Gitsune)

There is a legend that Murasaki Shikibu, authoress of 'The Tale of Genji' (*Genji Monogatari*), went to hell after she died. The reason is given that she committed the sin of *kyôgen kigo* (fictitious) error. The phrase is a most appropriate expression of the very essence of what Murasaki Shikibu wrote about.

Thus if Buddhist ethics are taken as a standard, a *kyôgen kigo* is some sort of fabulosity that deludes and corrupts the hearts of the masses. It is an anti-religious act of folly, the erratic words of a madman. Considered from the opposite viewpoint, it can also be said to mean fascinating stories that tell of not only the whole realm of human nobility and beauty, but of human foolishness and sadness as well.

5

We have wandered somewhat astray from our original purpose, but the point of all this is that this word *kyôgen*, pregnant with nuances of meaning, came to be used to refer to the stage art we know by that name some time after the Period of the Northern and Southern Dynasties (ended in 1393 a.d.).

On the other hand, in modern times, the word *kyôgen* has also come to mean a Kabuki script or play. Due to the general popularity of Kabuki, the average person tends to relate the word *kyôgen* to Kabuki perhaps more than to the classical comic theatre art we are concerned with here. Its most common use, therefore, is in such conversations a 'What *kyôgen* is playing at the Kabuki-za this month?' 'It's the complete *Chûshingura* (The Forty-Seven Ronin).' Here the

5. Manzo Nomura as the Mute, Mansaku Nomura as the Blind Man and Mannojo Nomura as the Cripple in 'The Handicapped Three' (Sannin Katawa)

6. Mannojo Nomura as Taro in 'A Rice Bale Mistaken for a Girl' (Yoneichi)

word means the program of Kabuki plays. From this same viewpoint, such Kabuki playwrights as Nanboku and Mokuami are called *kyôgen sakusha* in modern Japanese. And even today, there is a room in Kabuki theatre dressing room areas known as the Kyogen Sakusha Room. The people who inhabit this room today are those who are involved in such miscellane-

7. Keigoro Zenchiku as Narihira in 'The Poet
and the Rice Cakes' (Narihira Mochi)

ous literary activities as copying out parts
and acting as prompters.

In order to avoid confusion when referring to the classical comic theatre art, the

term Noh-Kyogen came into use to indicate that one is speaking about the Kyogen of the Noh drama rather than about the scripts or programs of Kabuki. But this term presents problems as well, because it also has two possible meanings. Using this term makes it sound as though Kyogen is subordinate to Noh. While this has some basis in historical fact, particularly during the days of the Tokugawa Shogunate (1603-1867), in recent years the art of Kyogen has come to be considered the theatre of the people and the very roots of Japanese humor. Thus it is distressing for it to be still considered no more than the *hors d'oeuvre* of Noh. The subordinating effect is one of the problems in the use of this term,

8. Motohide Izumi as the Gambler and Manzo Nomura as Emma, King of Hell in 'A Gambler Beats the King of Hell' (Bakuchi Jûô)

and the other is because it tends to sound as though it is referring to both Noh and Kyogen. Thus in very recent times, when referring to both Noh and Kyogen, the term 'Nogaku' has come into use, and Kyogen is simply called Kyogen. The intricacies of the Japanese language cause communication difficulties in any field from time to time, and while these difficulties sound rather petty to an outsider, they do indeed exist and must be coped with.

Fraternal Twins — Noh and Kyogen

From the historical point of view, it is an undeniable fact that Noh and Kyogen were originally an inseparable pair of theatrical forms. While they are absolutely identical in many aspects, they are entirely different in others, very much like a pair of fraternal twins.

10. Mannojo Nomura as the Kamamkura Man and Mansaku Nomura as the Kyoto Man in 'The Glue Fight' (Kôyaku Neri)

It was mentioned earlier that the term Nogaku includes both Noh and Kyogen, but this term has come into use only since the Meiji Period (1868-1912). Up through the Edo (or Tokugawa) Period, the term 'Sarugaku' was used.

The origins of Sarugaku date

◄ 9. Tokuro Miyake as the Persimmon Seller and Motohide Izumi, Ukon Miyake, Aizo Yamamoto and Heiroku Sano as the Worshippers in 'Hybrid Persimmons' (Awase-Gaki)

11

12. Manzo Nomura as the Thief and Mansaku Nomura as the Farmer in 'The Melon Thief' (Uri Nusubito)

back to the Nara Period (708-793) when its ancestor art called 'Sangaku' was imported from China. It seems that Sangaku was a popular variety show type of theatre that consisted of acrobatic stunts, juggling, and magic tricks, which had developed into a comic mime theatre style by the Heian Period (794-1185). And the name Sarugaku, by which it came to be known during the same period, seems to have been a phonemic mutation of the original Sangaku, which took advantage of the slight similarity of sound to add the association of the monkey (*saru*)—an animal that seems particularly fond of humorous mimicry.

Let us now take a look at the available information that gives us some idea of what constituted the comic mime pieces

◀11. Mannojo Nomura in the title role and Matasaburo Nomura as the Cripple in 'The Fake Deva King' (Niô)

of early Sarugaku. In Japan's earliest literary work on theatre titled 'A New Record of Sarugaku' (*Shin Sarugaku Ki*), written by Akihira Fujiwara around the middle of the 11th century, the author tells of a group of inferior government officials known as *toneri* performing such mimes as 'catching shrimp,' 'the mistakes of a country bumpkin on his first visit to the capital,' and 'a nun running around begging for diapers for her new baby.' Such skits as these were performed as entertainment in the courtyards of the mansions of the aristocracy during the latter part of the Heian Period. While they seem quite simple and even childish, hints of the budding spirit of theatrical satire can be seen here, admittedly dim but undeniably certain. This type of comic mime was clearly the mainstream of early Sarugaku.

Subsequently, during the early part of the Kamakura Period (1186-1333), groups of Sarugaku actors began to form

14. Takao Zenchiku, Juro Zenchiku and Tadashige Zenchiku as the Shysters and Motoyoshi Okura as the Country Man in 'The Six Statues' (Roku Jizō)

companies or troupes. Also other performing arts, such as the *jushi* and *ennen* dances in the temples and shrines, and the *dengaku* of the rural village planting and harvest ceremonies and festivals had developed over the centuries separately from Sarugaku.

Gradually the comic mime art was superceded by a song and dance art of more serious and profound content which

◀ 13. Manzo Nomura as the Shyster, Mannojo Nomura as the Country Man and Mannosuke Nomura as the Arbiter in 'The Tea Box' (Cha Tsubo)

15

15. Manzo Nomura as the Well-to-do Man in 'Visiting Hanago'
(Hanago)

16

later came to be known as Noh, and the comic skits of the older Sarugaku split away to develop into the dialogue theatre form we know as Kyogen. The dividing of the art into two clearcut separate forms of diametrically opposed character — the tragic, symbolistic song and dance drama of the Noh and the comic, representational dialogue drama of Kyogen — actually served as a mutual aid in development, and deepened their interdependent relationship as well. By the Muromachi Period (1392-1466), when father and son Kanami and Zeami brought the art of Sarugaku Noh to its lofty artistic level of perfection within a single generation, Kyogen had already been absorbed and integrated into the theatrical companies of Noh. From that time, throughout the Edo Period (1600-1867) and all the way

16. Mansaku Nomura as Kaiami, the Tea Priest, and Manzo Nomura as the Daimyo in 'Spring, Girls, and Sake' (Wakana)

17. Manzo Nomura as the Nenbutsu Priest and Tokuro Miyake as the Hokke Priest in 'A Religious Dispute' (Shûron)

to the present day, the programming style of Noh and Kyogen plays being performed alternately in any given presentation has been maintained.

The Age when Kyogen was Born

We will delve into the depths of the relationship between Noh and Kyogen in a later section. Therefore, let us pause here to consider the historical background from which Kyogen was born.

The Muromachi Period, which gave birth to the art of Kyogen, was the latter half of what we commonly speak of as the Middle Ages—a time of transition that saw both the inheritance and propagation of the ancient aristocratic culture

18. The late Tojiro Yama-moto as the Priest in 'The Dance of the God Jizo (Jizô Mai)

and the genesis of a modern plebeian culture. The warrior class seized the actual political power from the aristocracy, and proceeded toward the solidification of the foundations of a

19. Sensaku Shigeyama as the Blind Man and Yataro Okura as the Passer-by in 'The Moon-Viewing Blind Man' (Tsuki-mi Zato)

feudalistic society. At the same time, on the psychological and spiritual plane, the culture of the masses began to take on a certain characteristic form which became the source of Japanese tradition as we know it today. Throughout the centuries of natural calamity and interminable internecine hostility, the people learned to assuage their deep-seated feelings of fear and insecurity through belief in the power of a new Buddhism, which advocated a deep respect for matters concerning the spirit and the inner life. It was also this same period that gave birth to such arts as the tea ceremony, flower

21. Manzo Nomura as the Hokke Priest and Tokuro Miyake as the Parishoner in 'Sermon Wihtout Donation' (Fuse Nai Kyô)

20. Kitaro Wada as Akutaro the Drunkard and Heiroku Sano as his Uncle in 'Akutaro Reforms' (Akutarô)

arrangement, ink painting, and gardening with their high esthetic standards expressed in the words *wabi*, *sabi*, and *shibui* (terms which refer to the beauty of melancholy, decay, and astringency or restraint) that constitute the essence of uniquely Japanese styles of expression.

In the field of literature as well, all the aristocratic taste for elegance and delicacy of the late Heian Period was swept away in the wake of a new life force that was full of vigorous energy. And as is typical of any period of transition, there was also a strong general tendency toward retrogression to the culture of a more ancient period. In this case the phenomenon revealed itself in the form of retrospection on and nostalgia for the lost culture of the Monarchic Ages of the Nara (8th century) and early Heian periods.

Kyogen reflects the psychological and spiritual chaos of this time in which the old establishment had crumbled, but a new social order had not yet taken root.

23. Motosugu Okura as the Acolyte and Motoyoshi Okura as the Temple Maid in 'Drawing Water' (Ocha no Mizu or Mizu Kumi)

22. Manzo Nomura as the Priest and Tokuro Miyake as the Nun in 'The Crying Nun' (Naki Ama)

25

The Evolution of Kyogen

There is not sufficient space in these pages to present a detailed history of Kyogen, but let us take a look at the major trends in the evolution of the art to date. The establishment of strictly organized schools in both Noh and Kyogen came about in the early part of the Edo Period during the reign of the third Tokugawa Shogun, Iemitsu. The Tokugawa Shogunate designated Nogaku as the official property of the military class. This was done from feelings of rivalry with the Imperial Court and its private art of Gagaku. Nogaku performers (*shite* actors, *waki* actors, musicians, and Kyogen actors) were subsidized by either the government or by the head of a clan. The Okura and Sagi schools were under the direct support of the Shogunate,

25. Motohide Izumi in the title role of 'The Octopus' (Tako) ▶
24. Kosuke Nomura as the Child, Tokuro Miyake and Aizo Yamamoto as Kanazu Farmers in 'The Impudent Jizo Statue' (Kanazu Jizō)

but the Izumi school was patronized by the Tokugawa Clan of
Owari (present Aichi Prefecture) and the Maeda Clan of Kaga
(present Ishikawa Prefecture), and also served in the Imperial
Court. Both Noh and Kyogen experienced security during the
three hundred years of the Edo Period as highly aesthetic arts

26. Tokuro
Miyake as
the Nun in
'The Plum
Blossom
Hut' (Iori
no Ume)

patronized by the military class. This resulted in both
advantages and disadvantages. The establishment of a highly
refined and pure style is indeed on the plus side. However, the
resulting overly-rigid classification system and the strict old-
fachioned rules involved in promulgating these arts are strong

27. Chuichiro Zenchiku in the title role of 'Tsuen, the Tea Priest'
(Tsūen)

28. Matasaburo Nomura in the title role and Mansaku Nomura as the Travelling Priest in 'Yuzen, the Unskillful Umbrella Maker' (Yūzen)

disadvantages in many ways.

Along with the Meiji Restoration (1868) came the collapse of the old military government establishment, leaving Noh and Kyogen with no means of support and no one to back them. The actors split in all directions, and the world of Nogaku fell into a state of confusion. The almost total disappearance of the Sagi school today is due mainly to the confusion brought about by the Meiji Restoration. Thanks to the efforts of Tomomi Iwakura and his compatriots, Nogaku gradually began to show signs of a renaissance during the first ten years of the Meiji Period. The moving energy behind this renaissance from the world of Nogaku itself was provided by the Noh actors

31

◀

29. Tokuro Miyake as Taro in 'Unsuccessful Suicide with a Sickle' (Kamabara)
30. Mansaku Nomura as the Man with a Beard and Mannosuke Nomura as his wife in 'The Fortified Beard' (Hige Yagura) ▼

Minoru Umewaka and Kuro Hosho and the Kyogen actors Shoichi Miyake and Azuma Yamamoto. Both Noh and Kyogen found patrons among the new financial clique and the aristocrats, to take the place of the Shogunate and the clan leaders who had supported them in the past. Nogaku fluorished indeed under this new patronage, and it is thanks to the moneyed classes that we are able to see Noh and Kyogen today, but it is also unfortunate that even after the Meiji Period, it was the very nature of this patronage that kept Noh and Kyogen from being enjoyed by the general public for quite a long period of time.

Since humor is the main objective of Kyogen, Japanese society, in which the Confucian feudal ethics are still deeply ingrained, has given it unduely cold treatment, especially compared to its enthusiastic support of the 'serious' Noh. People who study Noh singing and dancing and the playing of its musical instruments, most industriously follow the printed texts and give a Noh play their full attention. These same people consider it normal and natural to begin chatting noisily with their friends, eating their lunches, and using the various

31. Yataro Okura as the Warrior Priest and Juro Zenchiku as the Younger Brother in 'The Hooting Warrior Priest' (Fukurô or Fukurô Yamabushi)

lobby facilities as soon as a Kyogen play begins, no matter how excellent or powerful the performance of the Kyogen actors on the stage may be.

It is only since the end of the Pacific War that Kyogen has really begun to flourish and that its true value has become generally enjoyed and appreciated. During the fifties it was finally recognized that Kyogen can stand on its own as a truly fine theatre art, independent and apart from the Noh. People who had never before seen anything other than modern plays and films have now begun both to attend performances of and take lessons in the techniques of Kyogen, bringing about an entirely new attitude toward the art.

Kyogen Scripts

Kyogen is a simple and native style of drama, as far as the subject matter presented is concerned. During the early generations, it was passed down only in the form of scenarios, as was

32. Chuichiro Zenchiku as Taro Kaja and Noriyasu Takai as the Master in 'Sinner by Lottery' (Kuji Zinin)

33. Yataro Okura as the Demon and Motoyoshi Okura as the
Woman in 'The Demon's Stepchild' (Oni no Mamako)

36

true of its brother art of the West—the Italian Commedia dell'-
Arte. In other words, only brief story outlines were preserved
and passed down. Thus the actual dialogue and movement was
improvised by the performers on the stage.

The very oldest of these scenarios in existence today are
found in a document titled the 'Tensho Kyogen Book,' which
was written during the 1570s. Let us take the scenario for 'An
Umbrella Instead of a Fan' (*Suehiro-Gari*; 93*) as an example
to illustrate the brevity and simplicity of the entries in this
document.

"A Daimyo appears and calls his servant. He tells the
servant to go the capital and buy the most expensive fan
(*suehiro*) he can find. The servant goes to the capital and
begins shouting about what he wants to buy. A Shyster appears
and sells him an umbrella instead. The Shyster also tells him

---

* *Editor's Note: Numerals in parentheses refer to the photos
relating to the play being mentioned.*

34.　Manzo Nomura as Emma, King of Hell, and Tokuro Miyake
　　as the Sinner in 'A Sinner with References' (Yao)

35. Yataro Okura as the Warrior Priest, Takao Zenchiku as the Shinto Priest, and Noriyasu Takai as the Tea Shop Owner in 'The Shinto Priest and the Warrior Priest' (Negi Yamabushi)

that if his master gets angry at him, he should sing this song, 'On Umbrella Mountain, on Umbrella Mountain, if other people open their umbrellas, I'll open my umbrella too.' The servant goes home. When the Master sees what the Servant has bought, he gets angry. He chases the Servant out of the house. Then the Servant begins singing and dancing. The Master listens and enjoys the song so much that he begins dancing too. Master and Servant dance together. The play ends with a sound from the flute."

This is the entire scenario for the play. The book has scenarios of this sort for one hundred and four different plays.

As generations went by, the repertoire grew larger, plots and dialogue became more clearly set, and the number of complete scripts also began to increase. There are more than

36. Koshiro Zenchiku as the Warrior Priest and Tadashige Zenchiku as the Acolyte (the actor playing the Crab is not identified) in 'The Warrior Priest and the Crab' (Kani Yamabushi)

37. Keigoro Zenchiku as the Warrior Priest, Takao Zenchiku as Taro Kaja, and Koshiro Zenchiku as the Master in 'The Snail' (Kagyû)

thirty volumes of complete scripts among the various schools that have come to light in modern times.

Classification of Plays

The total number of Kyogen plays that have been passed down to us today in the script collections comes to somewhere between four and five hundred. However, the total number of plays in the present active repertoire of the Okura and Izumi schools together comes to only 260. Strictly speaking, there are 180 in the Okura repertoire and 254 in that of the Izumi school. 174 of these are common to both schools, six are in the Okura school only and eighty are in only the Izumi school, bringing the grand total of plays in the present repertoire of both schools to 260.

These plays have been divided into several categories, depending on either the type of character designated as the *shite* (the term used to identify the major role in both Noh and Kyogen) or the overall theme of the piece. There are various discrepancies in these classifications depending on the school or the scholar writing about them, but the most common grouping system divides them into the following ten classifications: Celebratory (*waki*) pieces, Daimyo pieces, Taro Kaja pieces, Son-in-Law or Groom (*muko*) pieces, Woman (*onna*) pieces, Demon (*oni*) pieces, Warrior Priest (*yamabushi*) pieces,

38.   Manzo Nomura as the Warrior Priest and Mannojo Nomura as one of the Mushrooms in 'Mushrooms' (Kusabira)

Priest (*shukke*) pieces, Blind Man (*zatô*) pieces, and Miscellaneous or Group (*zô* or *atsume*) pieces.

Let us take a look at the tendencies and special characteristics of the pieces in terms of these ten classifications. Problems will, however, arise in cases where titles or classifications differ between the schools. For instance, the piece titled 'The Tricky Memory Trick' (*Bunzô*; 86, 87+88) is a case in point as it is classified as a Daimyo piece in the Okura school, but as a Taro Kaja piece in the Izumi school. Also 'Thunder' (*Kaminari*; 39) is the same in both schools, but its title is written in different characters. And there are cases of

39. Tojiro Yamamoto in the title role and his father the late Tojiro Yamamoto as the Quack Doctor in 'Thunder' (Kaminari)

40. Mannojo Nomura as Asahina and Mansaku Nomura as Emma, King of Hell in 'Asahina, the Warrior' (Asahina)

42. Tokuro Miyake as the Demon Father, Ukon Miyake as Tametomo, and Motohide Izumi as the Demon Princess in 'Neck Pulling' (Kubi Hiki)

◀ 41. Manzo Nomura as Taro Kaja in 'Shedding the Demon Shell' (Nuke-Gara)

title differences such as 'The Chrysanthemum' which is called *Bô-bô-gashira* in the Okura and *Kiku no Hana* in the Izumi school. (*Editor's Note: Such pieces have been given only one English title throughout the book*.) Thus in explaining the classifications, in the following pages, care has been taken to choose examples that have the same titles and are in the same classifications in both schools, but this has not always been possible. Thus when a piece has different titles, the Okura title has been given first with the Izumi title following immediately after it, both in parentheses, following the English title.

Celebratory (waki) Pieces   Kyogen is usually thought of as a theatre of humor and satire but these pieces bring forth very few laughs, as their subject matter is concentrated on felicitous ceremonies and the conferring of blessings.

43 + 44. Manzo Nomura and others as the Gourd Beaters and
Kosuke Nomura as the Gourd God in 'The Gourd Beaters'
(Hachi Tataki)

The term *waki* comes from the first group of Noh plays that are also referred to as God (*kami*) pieces. When a formal program of Noh is presented, it begins with the ceremonial piece title 'Okina' (a piece that is considered separate and apart from the other groupings due to its ceremonially sacred character). Next comes a Celebratory piece, then a Warrior Ghost (*shura*) piece, a Wig (*katsura*) piece, a Miscellaneous (*zatsu*) piece, and an End (*kiri*) piece. This five piece program was established during the Edo Period. On the formal program, Kyogen are presented, one each between the five pieces, making the number of Kyogen pieces on such a program come to four. Both 'Okina' and the Celebratory Noh pieces have for their themes prayers and thanksgiving for universal peace and prosperity and a rich and abundant harvest, as well as praise for the divinity and virtue of the deities. The Kyogen pieces that are chosen for presentation following the Celebratory Noh

pieces also have the conferring of blessings as their theme. Thus they have come to be designated by the same name – Celebratory (*waki*) Kyogen.

In these pieces, appear such gods as Daikoku with his magic hammer; Ebisu with his sea bream and his fishing pole; or Bishamon who is dressed in armor and a helmet and carries a halberd–gods who had just begun to gain large numbers of believers during the Muromachi Period. When such a deity

45. Mannojo
    Nomura as
    the Demon
    and
    Mansaku
    Nomura as
    the Woman
    in 'A
    Demon in
    Love'
    (Setsubun)

appears, he explains why he is auspicious, tells the history of
his origins, and bestows blessings on all the people, presenting a
bright and happy world of practical faith. At the end of these
pieces, such formal dances as a *sandan-no-mai* or a *mai-bataraki*
are performed, accompanied by an orchestra and a chorus,
making them far more formal in style than the average Kyogen.
'The God of Happiness' (*Fuku no Kami*; 94), 'Ebisu and
Daikoku' (*Ebisu Daikoku*), 'Ebisu and Bishamon' (*Ebisu*

Bishamon), 'Daikoku and the Poets' (*Daikoku Renga*), 'The God Bishamon and the Poem' (*Bishamon Renga*), 'The Gourd God and Taro' (*Fukube no Shin*), 'The Spirit of Pine Resin' (*Matsu Yani*; 92), 'The Saké Container' (*Tsutsu Sasae*) are of this type, and are often referred to as Happiness God (*Fukushin*) pieces, as a separate division of the Celebratory pieces.

Another type in this category is the Wealthy Man (*kahô-mono*) pieces—'An Umbrella Instead of a Fan' (*Suehiro-Gari*; 93), 'Fans of Mistaken Identity' (*Mejika*), Aso Has His Hair Fixed' (*Asô*), 'Three Poles' (*Sanbon no Hashira*), 'Hiding the Hat' (*Kakure-Gasa*), 'The Magic Drum Stick' (*Takara no Tsuchi*), and 'Armor on Paper' (*Yoroi* or *Yoroi Haramaki*). The bulk of these pieces are about mistakes made by Taro Kaja when his Master sends him to the capital to buy something he

46. **Tokuro Miyake as the Blind Man and Motohide Izumi as his Wife in 'Blindness, Sight and Blindness Again' (Kawakami)**

47. Manzo Nomura as the Blind Man in 'Blindness, Sight and Blindness Again' (Kawakami)

51

48. Motohide Izumi as Kanaoka and Mansaku Nomura as his
Wife in 'Kanaoka, the Love-Crazed Painter' (Kanaoka)

49. Yataro Okura as Taro Kaja in 'The Capricious Magic Fish Hook' (Tsuri-Bari)

is not familiar with and is thus cheated out of his money by a Shyster. But the Master is always designated as a Wealthy Man, as opposed to the average Master in other Kyogen. Here the very wealth of the Master is considered auspicious and in each case, a type of song and dance called a *hayashi-mono* is used by the servant to get himself back into the good graces of his master after committing his foolish mistake, providing an additional celebratory note in their reconciliation.

One more type in this category is the Farmer (*hyakushō*) pieces. Here a farmer from a certain part of the country meets a farmer from another part of the country, both on their way to the capital to pay their annual taxes. When they reach the mansion of the Tax Collector, they are asked to accompany the presentation of their taxes with poems, the history and background of their respective products, or the recitation of the names of things they have brought, done in rhythm. This type includes

'Late Taxes' (*Mochi-Zake*), 'Three Farmers' (*Sannin-Bu*), 'One Hat For Two' (*Matsu Yuzuriha*), 'Seaweed and Persimmons' (*Kobu Kaki*), 'Two Words for Goose' (*Gan Karigane*), and 'Laughs After Taxes' (*Tsukushi no Oku*; 97). Most of these pieces end with such felicitous Endings (*tome*)

50 + 51. Kosuke Nomura as Igui, Mannojo Nomura as the Friend of Igui, and Manzo Nomura as the Fortune Teller in 'Igui, the Disappearing Boy' (Igui)

52. Keigoro Zenchiku as the Traveller and Yataro Okura as
    Taro Kaja in 'The Letter I' (I-Moji)

as a *sandan-no-mai*, a Song(*utai*) Ending, a Flute(*shagiri*) Ending,
or a Laugh (*warai*) Ending, to stress their celebratory nature.

The reason for the inclusion of the Farmer pieces in the
Celebratory category is because in Japan the farmer has always
been considered the nation's greatest treasure; and because of
the fact that when the farmer appears, he always begins his
introductory speech with, "In this felicitous age of ours in
which all is at peace in the world. . ." On the other hand, there
are those scholars like Akihira Sugiura, for example, who
stated in his book 'The Literature of the Age of Civil Strife'
(*Sengoku Ransei no Bungaku*), "Any farmer who was stupid
enough to enjoy paying his taxes must certainly have lived
during the tranquil days of the Tokugawa Period, or if he is
from some earlier period, the performers must certainly have
been trying their best to curry favor with the politically

powerful men in their audiences." Thus interpretation of this
type of pieces presents a number of problems.

The one Farmer piece that is an exception to the rule is 'The
Sado Fox' (*Sado-Gitsune*; 95+96). It is a unique piece in
which the paying of taxes and the proclaiming of universal
peace are played down to give way to the humor inherent in
the common human traits of vanity and the naive desire to
over-stretch oneself, along with the corruption of the Tax
Collector.

There are also Celebratory pieces that deal with quarrels
between tradesmen—'Pots and Drums' (*Nabe Yatsu Bachi*; 90+

91) and 'The Race of the Horse and the Cow' (*Gyûba*; 118)—
as well as those in which craftsmen, travelling entertainers, and
spirits of plants appear.

Daimyo Pieces   Most of the categories, other than the
Celebratory pieces, take their titles from the name of the major
role in the play. Thus as the name of this category indicates,
the *shite* of these pieces are all Daimyo. These are not the
grand lords of the Edo Period who held fiefs of more than one
million *koku* (one *koku* is equal to 5.119 U.S. bushels) annual
yield. This fact must be carefully kept in mind, for while it is
true that there are facets of Kyogen that reflect the social
conditions of the times in which the lower classes were seizing
power from their superiors, Kyogen was in no way such a
daring criticism of the statesmen of the day who had succeeded

◀ 53.   Tokuro Miyake as Taro and Motohide Izumi as the Wife of
Taro in 'The Stone God' (Ishigami)

  54.   Manzo Nomura as the Drunkard in 'The Baby's Mother's
(Hôshi ga Haha)

in establishing the strong Shogunate-Clan government.

The Daimyo of Kyogen are medieval land owners whose property consists of a few privately owned fields and who keep only a minimum number of retainers in their service. This does not mean that they should be played as countrified warriors. On the contrary, the Kyogen Daimyo has a unique and distinctive style of his own that has been refined on the stage for hundreds of years, which has very little in common with either the Edo Period clan chiefs or the rural village lords of medieval days (both of whom were designated by the term *daimyô*).

The Kyogen Daimyo strides majestically on to the stage wearing a tall stiff black hat called an *eboshi* and a formal cloak known as a *suô*, and he usually begins the piece by announcing himself in a loud resonant voice as "The well-

55. Mannojo Nomura as Taro and Mansaku Nomura as his Wife in 'Cautious Bravery' (Chigiri-Ki)

56 + 57.   Yagoro Zenchiku as Oko in 'The Trial Rehearsal' (Oko
Sako)

known Daimyo," or "A Daimyo who hails from a country far
away." The incidents in which these Daimyo are involved are
generally the direct result of their own blunders that are
brought about by their illiteracy, ignorance, foolishness, simple-
mindedness, or crudeness. Thus while they have a relatively
exalted social position and behave with a suitable level of
arrogance, an inner lowness of character is exposed at the same
time which makes them objects of laughter. This never reaches
the level of true satire, but rather, in the majority of cases, one
finds oneself ultimately identifying with the general lighthearted-
edness or magnanimity of the Daimyo on the stage. Thus it is
no doubt that the Edo Period Daimyo and warriors were
able to fully enjoy the presentation of Kyogen Daimyo, no
matter how ridiculously or how sarcastically the actor performed the role, without feeling in any way that the sarcasm was
aimed at themselves. This means that if there was any element

58. Sensaku Shigeyama as the Poet and Chusaburo Shigeyama as the Wife in 'The Winnow Basket Hat' (Mi Kazuki)

59. Chuichiro Zenchiku as Dondaro, Sengoro Shigeyama as the Wife and Keigoro Zenchiku as the Mistress in 'Dondaro's Method for Handling Women' (Dondarô)

of outspoken satirical intent in the early days when Kyogen originated, it had declined considerably by the time the art reached its present form.

There are 20 Daimyo pieces in the Okura school and 15 in the Izumi school. The fifteen pieces of the Izumi school are the same as those of the Okura School. They are 'A Man Poses as a Sword' (*Awataguchi*), 'Hired for a Riddle' (*Ima Mairi*), 'The Iruma River. (*Iruma-Gawa*; 75), 'The Monkey Skin Quiver' (*Utsubo-Zaru*; 80), 'Wrestling with a Mosquito' (*Ka-Zumô*;

60. Keigoro Zenchiku as the Son-in-Law and Yagoro Zenchiku
as the Father-in-Law in 'The Water Throwing Son-in-Law'
(Mizu Kake Muko)

76, 77+78), 'A Goose and a Pebble' (*Gan Tsubute*), 'Keep
Quiet and Keep Out of Trouble' (*Kinya*), 'The Riddle Umbrella'
(*Shuku-Gasa*), 'Black Crocodile Tears' (*Sumi Nuri*), 'The

61. Tojiro Yamamoto as Jiro Kaja and Noritoshi Yamamoto as Taro Kaja in 'The Fox Mound' (Kitsune-Zuka)

Daimyo and the Bush Clover Blossoms' (*Hagi Daimyô*; 83), 'Nose-Pulling Sumo' (*Hana-Tori-Zumô*), 'Wrestling by the Book' (*Fu-Zumô* or *Fumi-Zumô*), 'Two Daimyos' (*Futari Daimyô*; 84 +85), 'The Goose Stealing Daimyo' (*Gan Daimyô*), and 'The Demon-Faced Tile' (*Oni-Gawara*). And the remaining five in the category in the Okura school also exist in the Izumi school repertoire, but are included in the Taro Kaja or the Miscellaneous categories. They are 'The Seaweed Seller' (*Kobu Uri*). 'Buaku, the Living Ghost' (*Buaku*; 81+82), 'The Fuji Pine' (*Fuji Matsu*), 'The Tricky Memory Trick' (*Bunzô*; 86,87+88), 'The Chrysanthemum' (*Bô-bô-Gashira* or *Kiku no Hana*). All except for three pieces—'Keep Quiet and Keep Out of Trouble' (*Kinya*), 'A Goose and a Pebble' (*Gan Tsubute*), and 'Two Daimyos' (*Futari Daimyô*; 84+85)— have the servant Taro Kaja in the secondary role (called the *ado* in Kyogen). Taro Kaja is generally sent out to buy something or other, or to find someone to hire as a new servant for the Daimyo. The new

63. Ukon Miyake as the Groom, Tokuro Miyake as the Father ▶ of the Groom, Kitaro Wada as the Father-in-Law, and Hiroshi Wada as Taro Kaja in 'Two People in One Hakama' (Futari-Bakama)

servants are mostly good at sumo wrestling, and the Daimyo wrestles with them to test their skill. There are also pieces which deal with incidents that happen during the Daimyo's stay in the capital on business. Also three of these pieces deal with hunting excursions—'The Monkey Skin Quiver' (*Utsubo-Zaru*; 80), 'Keep Quiet and Keep Out of Trouble' (*Kinya*), and 'A Goose and a Pebble' (*Gan Tsubute*)—in which the Daimyo announces himself as "the well-know archer."

Taro Kaja Pieces   Kyogen that have the servant called Taro Kaja as their major character (*shite*). This is the largest category in the repertoire. And when the Miscellaneous pieces and the Daimyo pieces in which he appears are included, it becomes clear why Taro Kaja is considered the most typically Kyogenlike of all the characters who appear throughout the entire repertoiire. And this seems only natural when considered in light of the etymology of his name. Taro is such a common Japanese man's name that it is used as Everyman in a similar

Juro Zenchiku as the Groom and Yataro Okura as the Boat-
man (Father-in-Law) in 'The Groom in the Boat' (Funa-
Watashi Muko)

way to the use of Jack in the West. And *Kaja* (pronounced
kanja outside of Kyogen) is the term for a boy who has just
celebrated his coming of age. Thus it is used as a general term
for 'young man' or 'servant.'

In his book titled 'Townspeople' (*Machishû*), Tatsusaburo
Hayashiya takes Taro Kaja's dialogue from 'The Crown
Prince's Halberd' (*Taishi no Te-boko*) as an example. Taro Kaja
says, "My house is such a run down shack that whenever it

65 + 66. Tojiro Yamamoto as Jiro Kaja and Noboru Nakajima as Taro Kaja in 'Tied to a Stick' (Bō Shibari)

rains three drops outside, we get ten drops inside, so that my wife and children have to huddle in the corners to keep dry." Based upon this, Hayashiya explains, "Taro Kaja was a man of the servant class living in the midst of Kyoto. . . It was from this lifestyle that the satire concerning Taro Kaja was born with such poignant reality. Thus it is no exaggeration to state that Kyogen is a direct expression of the lower class of Kyotoites." There is an interesting point made here, as Taro Kaja lived right next door to merchants and craftsmen, and can thus be compared to the white collar worker in modern society who lives in the giant housing complexes known as *danchi*. In other words, he is a reflection of the universal man of the people—an Everyman.

The reason for Taro Kaja's being chased off or scolded at the end of the bulk of the pieces in which he appears is because of his inadept handling of the situation in which he is placed or the responsbility he has been given. But his mishandling is never done maliciously. There are many cases in which Taro Kaja shows great love and respect for his Master. There are times when Taro Kaja gets scolded for the mistakes of his Master. While Taro Kaja is always basically a good man at heart, he tends to cause his Master a great deal of grief by carelessly getting his orders confused as in 'The Sound of Bells' (*Kane no Ne*; 73), by trying to bluff his way through a situation in which he has been very cowardly as in 'The Brave Coward' (*Sora Ude*), by making blunders due to his habit of over-drinking as in 'The Half-Delivered Gift' (*Kirokuda*; 69+70), 'Shedding the Demon Shell' (*Nuke-Gara*; 41), and 'The Dropped Gift' (*Suô-Otoshi*; 72), by causing an uproar through stealing saké from his Master's storehouse and getting hopelessly drunk as in 'Tied to a Stick' (*Bô Shibari*; 65+66) and 'Piped in Saké' (*Hi no Sake*; 71), and by lying to get out of being sent

68. Tokuro Miyake as Taro Kaja and Motohide Izumi as Jiro Kaja in 'The Delicious Fatal Poison' (Busu)

◄67. Yataro Okura as Taro Kaja and Sensaku Shigeyama as the Saké Shop Owner in 'Catching Plovers' (Chidori)

69 + 70. Tokuro Miyake as Taro Kaja and Motohide Izumi as
the Tea Shop Owner in 'The Half-Delivered Gift' (Kirokuda)

out on an errand as in 'Inherited Cramps' (*Shibiri*) and 'A Demon For Better Working Conditions' (*Shimizu*). But no matter how lazy he may be, Taro Kaja always comes off in the end as a lovable character. In 'Catching Plovers' (*Chidori*; 67), Taro Kaja manages to trick a saké shop owner out of just one more barrel of saké for his Master, in spite of the large standing bill that has already been run up, with his clever stories and sharp wit. This shows a vigorous vitality and a deep worldly wisdom. Comparatively strong resistence to the authority of his Master is shown only in 'Shido Hogaku, the Horse' (*Shidô Hôgaku*; 62).

In the Okura school, there are 28 Taro Kaja pieces and 45 in the Izumi school. The following are the 24 pieces that are common to both schools—'Chapped Fest'(*Akagari*), 'The Sound of Bells'(*Kane no Ne*;73), 'The Fox Mound'(*Kitsune-Zuka*;61),'The

71. Manzo Nomura as Taro Kaja and Mansaku Nomura as Jiro
Kaja in 'Piped-In Sake' (Hi no Sake)

Half-Delivered Gift'(*Koirokuda*; 69+70), 'The Mimic' (*Kuchi Mane*), 'The Blessing Transfer' (*Kurama Mairi*), 'Roasting Chestnuts'(*Kuri Yaki*), "Three Tangerines on a Branch' (*Kôji*), 'Shido Hogaku, the Horse' (*Shidô Hôgaku*; 62), 'Inherited Cramps' (*Shibiri*), 'The Pine Branch and the Sword' (*Shinbai*), 'The Dropped Gift' (*Suô Otoshi*; 72), 'The Brave Coward'(*Sora Ude*), 'Sword Stealing' (*Tachi Bai* or *Tachi Ubai*), 'Catching Plovers' (*Chidori;* 'A Strange Evolution' (*Nariagari*), 'Rope Twisting' (*Nawa Nai*; 74), 'Horizontal Singing' (*Ne Ongyoku*; 79), 'The Flower Quarrel' (*Hana Arasoi*), 'The Delicious Fatal Poison' (*Busu*; 68), 'A Pronunciation Problem' (*Fune Funa*), 'Two to Deliver One Letter' (*Fumi Ninai*), 'Tied to a Stick' (*Bô Shibari*; 65+66), and 'Sakka, the Thief, (*Sakka*). There are also 'How to Cut Sea-Perch' (*Suzuki-Bôchô*) and 'Igui, the Dissappearing Boy' (*Igui*; 50+51) which are included in the Miscellaneous category by the Izumi school, 'The Chrysthemum' (*Bô-bô-Gashira* or *Kiku no Hana*) and 'The Fuji Pine' (*Fuji Matsu*) which the Okura school places in the Daimyo category, as well as 'Hiding the Badger' (*Kakushi-Danuki*) and 'Post or Person?' (*Kui Ka Hito Ka*) which exist only in the Izumi school.

In the Okura school this category is referred to as Small Landowner (*shômyô*) pieces. This indicates that the Masters in

72. Yagoro Zenchiku as Taro Kaja and Keigoro Zenchiku as the Master in 'The Dropped Gift' (Suô Otoshi)

73. Manzo Nomura as Taro Kaja in 'The Sound of Bells' (Kane no Ne)

the secondary (*ado*) roles of these pieces are far less wealthy than the Daimyo. Thus the name was most likely hit upon to point out the contrast between these and the Daimyo pieces, even though the major role (*shite*) is Taro Kaja.

In many Taro Kaja pieces, a second servant named Jiro Kaja appears. He is both a subordinate to Taro Kaja and often serves as his alterego. In such pieces as 'Tied to a Stick' (*Bô Shibari*; 65+66), 'The Delicious Fatal Poison' (*Busu*; 68), and 'Two to Deliver One Letter' (*Fumi Ninai*), both servants work together with interesting rhythms and related textures and a feeling of mutual good will.

Son-in-Law or Groom (muko) Pieces This category divides into three sections—First Ceremonial Visit (*muko iri*) pieces, Son-in-Law Choosing (*muko tori*) pieces, and Married Couple (*fûfu*) pieces.

The First Ceremonial Visit was a medieval custom in which a groom would make a formal visit to the home of his new

75. Sensaku Shigeyama as the Daimyo and Sengoro Shigeyama as the Man from Iruma in 'The Iruma River' (Iruma-Gawa)

◀ 74. Manzo Nomura as Taro Kaja, Mannosuke Nomura as the Old Master and Matasaburo Nomura as the New Master in 'Rope Twisting' (Nawa Nai)

76, 77 + 78. Tokuro Miyake as the Daimyo and Motohide Izumi as the Mosquito in 'Wrestling with a Mosquito' (Ka-zumô)

79. Manzo Nomura as Taro ▶ Kaja and Mansaku Nomura as the Master in 'Horizontal Singing' (Ne Ongyoku)

father-in-law. Incidents that happen on this celebratory occasion are handled here.

The Groom (*shite*) appears wearing a kimono with broad red and white horizontal stripes (*dan noshime*), a formal cloak called a *suô*, and a hard black hat of a peculiar triangular shape know as a *samurai eboshi*. In a nervously serious voice, he announces himself, "I am a new groom, the joy of my father-in-law." He brings gifts of food and wine, lending a definite celebratory note to the humor about to break forth due to this once-in-a-lifetime ceremony. The humor comes from the confusion brought about by the ignorance of this young man who is uninformed concerning the proper protocol for carrying out the ceremony. Pieces of this type include 'The Pocketed Groom' (*Kaichû Muko*), 'The Rooster Groom' (*Niwatori*

Muko), 'The Groom with a Leather Loin Cloth' (*Hisshiki Muko*), 'Two People in One Hakama' (*Futari-Bakama*; 63), 'The Groom in the Boat' (*Funa-Watashi Muko*; 64), 'The Butcherknife Groom' (*Hôchô Muko*), 'The Rhythmical Groom' (*Ongyoku Muko*), 'The Groom and the Saké Jug' (*Taru Muko*), 'The Paper Folding Groom' (*Origami Muko*), 'The Groom from Kurama' (*Kurama Muko*), 'The Groom from Echigo' (*Echigo*

80.
Sensaku
Shigeyama
as the
Daimyo,
Sengoro
Shigeyama
as the
Monkey
Trainer,
Koshiro
Zenchiku
as Taro
Kaja, and
Keiji
Matsushita
as the
Monkey in
'The
Monkey
Skin
Quiver'
(Utsubo-
Zaru)

Muko), and 'The Grandson Groom' (*Mago Muko*). In these pieces, Fathers-in-Law, Wives, and Friends, who teach the proper (or more often the improper) etiquette, appear in the secondary roles (*ado*).

There are just three Son-in-Law Choosing pieces—'Groom with Prompter' (*Yawata no Mae*), 'Counting Dice Spots' (*Sai no Me*), and 'The Water Horn Groom' (*Kakusui*). Each of these pieces begins with a Rich Man putting up a signboard advertising for a Groom for his Daughter. 'Groom with Prompter' (*Yawata no Mae*) ends in failure for the Groom, but the othe two end with the Groom trying to run away from the ugly Daughter, as in 'The Capricious Magic Fish Hook' (*Tsuri-Bari*; 49). There is one more piece of this type in the Izumi school called 'Ebisu and Bishamon' (*Ebisu Bishamon*), but it is included in the Celebratory (*waki*) category due to the appearance of deities.

'The Repentant Husband' (*Morai Muko*), 'The Water Throwing Son-in-Law' (*Mizu Kake Muko*), and 'Rice Cakes Called Okadayu' (*Okadayû*) all deal with love between a couple who have been married for some time, and conflict with the Father-in-Law. Thus it may actually have been better to include them in the next category.

Woman (onna) Pieces   As the name of this category

81 + 82. Yagoro Zenchiku as Buaku, Manzo Nomura as the Master, and Keigoro Zenchiku as Taro Kaja in 'Buaku,

indicates, these are plays in which Women (played by male actors) appear. However, they do not generally take the major role *shite*). The only Kyogen pieces in which the *shite* role is a woman are the three special pieces, 'The Aged Nun and Bikusada' (*Bikusada*), 'The Plum Blossom Hut' (*Iori no Ume*; 26) and 'The Badger's Belly Drum' (*Tanuki no Hara Tsuzumi*). The *shite* in all of these are aged nuns. This is, of course, a direct contrast to the Noh, where the Wig or Woman (*katsura*) pieces, which have elegantly fascinating women in their *shite* roles, are considered the most important and most typical category of the entire art.

While the women of Kyogen are relegated to supporting roles, they never fail to leave a strong impression. As mentioned above, in the case of Married Couple pieces, there is a great deal of overlap between this and the previous category. In 'Unsuccessful Suicide with a Sickle' (*Kamabara*; 29), 'The Trial

the Living Ghost' (Buaku)

Rehearsal' (*Oko Sako* or *Uchizata*; 56+57), 'The Fortified Beard' (*Hige Yagura*; 30+99), and 'The Stutter' (*Domori*), the wives seem to be pioneers of extremist women's liberation who never even give a man a fighting chance to be a man. On the other hand, there are wives who advocate women's rights in the opposite direction by showing inordinately deep love for their husbands, in such pieces as 'The Stone God' (*Ishigami*; 53), 'A Bad Wife is Like a Bad Penny' (*Inabadô*), 'The Man and the Mirror' (*Kagami Otoko*), 'Kanaoka, the Love-Crazed Painter' (*Kanaoka*; 48), and 'Visiting Hanago' (*Hanago*; 15). There are also charming wives like the one in 'The Winnow Basket Hat' (*Mi Kazuki*; 58).

Different from the situations handled in pieces concerning master-servant relationships or demons and animals, this category deals with love between married couples, presenting a more direct expression of the joys and sorrows of human life with a strong flavor of realism.

83.
Manzo
Nomura as
the Daimyo
and
Mannosuke
Nomura as
Taro Kaja
in 'The
Daimyo
and the
Bush Clover
Blossoms'
(Hagi
Daimyô)

84 + 85. Noritada and Noritoshi Yamamoto as the Two Daimyos and Tojiro Yamamoto as the Passer-by in 'Two Daimyos' (Futari Daimyô)

86.

The last type of play in the Woman category is the Ugly Woman (*shûjo*) pieces. Since they deal with the search for a new wife, they are also called Bride Searching (*Môshi-Zuma*) pieces, and include 'The Letter I' (*I Moji*; 52), '2918' (*Niku-Jûhachi*), and 'The Capricious Magic Fish Hook' (*Tsuri-Bari*; 49). Here a man goes to pray for a wife and is given an auspicious oracle in a dream, which tells him how to find the new wife the deity has chosen for him. But when he sees her unspeakably ugly face, he runs off crying for mercy with his new wife close at his heels.

Demon (oni) Pieces Just as women, who are generally considered to be the weaker sex, are presented as brawny and robust in Kyogen, demons, who are generally thought to be strong and frightening, are weak and good-hearted. Kyogen demons are of many types, ranging from the one from Horai Island in 'A Demon in Love' (*Setsubun*; 45), to those who live on Inaba Plain in 'Neck Pulling' (*Kubi Hiki*; 42), 'Thunder' (*Kaminari*; 39) in the piece of that name, and Emma, the King of Hell with his demon retainers.

Emma, the King of Hell, is the only demon to appear in more than one piece. He always comes out to the Crossing of the Six Roads to catch sinners and chase them down to hell, but the sinners always manage to force him to show them the road to Paradise instead. Emma appears in the *shite* role only

86, 87 + 88. The late Tojiro Yamamoto as the Master in 'The Tricky Memory Trick' (Bunzô)

in 'A Sinner With References' (*Yao*; 34), and in the *ado* role in 'Asahina, the Warrior' (*Asahina*, 40), 'Seirai, the Hawk Keeper and Emma, the King of Hell' (*Seirai*; 119), 'Bakuro, the Horse Trainer' (*Bakurô*), and 'A Gambler Beats the King of Hell' (*Bakuchi Jûô*; 8). The former three pieces are common to both schools, but the latter two are only in the Izumi school.

Warrior Priest (yamabushi) Pieces   The Warrior Priests were mountaineering ascetics who learned the Way of Buddha through a long period of strict austerities deep in the most impenetrable of all mountain areas. Their sect was originally a an off-shoot from Tantric Buddhism, but by medieval times, it had developed into a unique set of beliefs that had adopted aspects of popular folk religions and Shintoism. They were semi-lay priests in nature, and they spent their time wandering about the country, specializing in the chanting of potent prayers and incantations. They dressed in pretentiously

pompous costumes, cast secret spells, and made grandiloquent
claims, but in actual fact, they often failed in their attempts to
carry out their claims, and became the object of taunts and
sarcasm. Thus they appear in such Kyogen pieces as 'The
Warrior Priest and the Crab' (*Kani Yamabushi*; 36), 'The Shinto
Priest and the Warrior Priest' (*Negi Yamabushi*; 35), 'Mushrooms' (*Kusabira*; 38), 'The Dog and the Warrior Priest' (*Inu
Yamabushi*), 'The Hooting Warrior Priest' (*Fukurô* or *Fukurô*

89.
Tokuro
Miyake as
the
Emperor of
China and
Motohide
Izumi as
the
Japanese
Sumo
Wrestler in
'Chinese
Sumo'
(Tōjin-
Zumô)

Yamabushi; 31), 'The Persimmon Thief' (*Kaki Yamabushi*), and 'The Back-Straightening Prayer' (*Koshi Inori*). Kyogen Warrior Priests demonstrate truly effective powers of enchantment only in 'The Snail' (*Kagyû*; 37) and 'The Lunch Thief' (*Tsuto Yamabushi*).

Demon and Warrior Priest pieces are not meant to be a criticism of authority, but are aimed at simply expressing a humor of the type found in fairy tales and comic books.

90 + 91. Manzo Nomura as the Seller of Earthenware Pots and Mansaku Nomura as the Seller of Drums in 'Pots and Drums' (Nabe Yatsu Bachi)

92. Keigoro Zenchiku in the▶ title role of 'The Spirit of Pine Resin' (Matsu Yani)

Priest (shukke) Pieces   The Kamakura and Muromachi periods were the golden age of religion in Japan. The Demon pieces explained above were a sort of turning inside out of the yearing for the paradise promised by the Jodo Sect and the fear of hell. While the medieval age was a period that saw the birth of numerous new sects of Buddhism and was the quickening period for a new sense of values, it was also a time of insecurity, confusion, and disorder. These social conditions produced not only highly virtuous and sincere priests, but also men who became priests due to failure in business or the necessity to escape from some uncomfortable situation, and who simply travelled about the country begging for a living in priestly guise.

The Priest category is the third largest group of Kyogen after the Taro Kaja and Woman categories. 'Sermon Without Donation' (*Fuse Nai Kyô*; 21), 'A Religious Dispute' (*Shûron*; 17), and 'The Name Stealing River' (*Natori-Gawa*) are the masterpieces of the group. The illiteracy, greed, lust, arrogance and prejudice of these vagrant priests is also skillfully delineated in 'The Forgotten Boat Fare' (*Satsuma-no-Kami*), 'The Dance of the God Jizo' (*Jizô Mai*; 18), 'Almost a Priest' (*Roren*), 'Priest Angerless Honesty' (*Hara Tatezu*), 'The Crying Nun' (*Naki Ama*; 22), and 'The Nun Nyakuichi's Revenge' (*Nyakuichi*).

Among the Priest pieces, there is a group of plays that has an Acolyte (*shinbochi*– a young priest who has only recently taken his vows) in the *shite* role. It includes such pieces as 'The Mixed-up Acolyte' (*Hone Kawa*), 'Forbidden Blossoms' (*Hana Ori*), 'Drawing Water' (*Ocha no Mizu* or *Mizu Kumi*: 23),

Blind Man (zatô) Pieces   During the Muromachi Period, four official titles were established for blind men. They were, in order of rank, *kengyô*, *bettô*, *kôtô*, and *zatô*. Blind *biwa* (Japanese lute) troubadours were generally referred to by the title *zatô* in the early days, but as time went on, this title came to be used to refer to any blind man with his head shaved who made his living by playing the *biwa*, the *koto*, or the *shamisen* while singing or narrating ancient tales, or who was a professional masseur or acupuncturist. And finally *zatô* became the generic term for any person who had lost his sight. It is thought that all early vocal and instrumental entertainers were blind priests. And the fact that this postion of power and authority in the performing arts was maintained by blind priests throughout the middle ages and into modern times is clearly reflected in the frequent performing of the narrative 'Tales of the Heike' by the *zatô* who appear in Kyogen.

'Hakuyo, the Blind Biwa Borrower' (*Hakuyô*), 'Plunk!

93. Noritada Yamamoto as the Master and Tojiro Yamamoto as Taro Kaja in 'An Umbrella Instead of a Fan' (Suehiro-Gari)

94. Yataro Okura in the title role of 'The God of Happiness'
(Fuku no Kami)

Click!' (*Dobu Kachiri*), 'Blind Man's Football' (*Mari Zatô*),
'The Blind Man and the Monkey' (*Saru Zatô*), and 'The Deaf
Man and the Blind Man, (*Kikazu Zatô*) are Priest pieces that
exist in the repertoires of both schools.

Miscellaneous (zô) or Group (atsume) Pieces The remaining plays that do not fit comfortably into any of the above
categories are grouped together as Miscellaneous pieces by the
Izumi school (40 pieces) and as Group pieces by the Okura
school (25 pieces). Placement in this category by no means
indicates that a piece is without distinction or of lesser value
than those of other categories. On the contrary, many of the
pieces here are among the most popular of all Kyogen, and
there are also those here that demand a very high level of

▲ 95 + 96. Chusaburo Shigeyama as the Farmer from Sado, Chuichiro
Zenchiku as the Tax Collector, and Koshiro Zenchiku as the
Farmer from Echigo in 'The Sado Fox' (Sado-Gitsune)

▼ 97. Mannojo and Mansaku Nomura as the Farmers from Tanba and
Tsukushi, and Manzo Nomura as the Tax Collector in 'Laughs
After Taxes' (Tsukushi no Oku)

technique to perform and are considered the most important pieces in the entire repertoire.

The Dwarf Tree Thief' (*Bonsan*); the Bandit (*sanzoku*) pieces—'The Cowardly Bandits' (*Fumi Yamadachi*), and 'Skinny Pine' (*Kintozaemon* or *Yase Matsu*); the Shyster (*suppa*) pieces—'The Tea Box' (*Cha Tsubo*; 13), 'The Hadicapped Three' (*Sannin Katawa*; 5), and 'The Fake Deva King' (*Niô*; 11); and the Pedigree Dispute (*yuisho arasoi*) pieces—'The Glue Fight' (*Koyaku Neri*; 10). There are also several pieces that are indeed purely miscellaneous in character—'Learning the Alphabet'(*I-Ro-Ha*), 'The Brother Fight' (*Shatei*), 'How to Cut Sea-Perch'(*Suzuki-Bôchô*), 'A Cat Killed for a Chicken'(*Keimyô*), Sightseer-zaemon' (*Kenbutsu-zaemon*), and 'The Fruit War' (*Ko-no-Mi Arasoi*).

Dance Kyogen (mai kyogen) pieces These are very special pieces. They take the dramaturgical form of the Phantasmal (*mugen*) group of Noh plays in which a travelling priest (the *waki* or secondary role) questions a local person (the *ai* or entr'acte) concerning the legends surrounding some person or entity that had formerly lived in the area. Then as the priest prays for the departed soul of the person in the story that had been related to the place, its ghost (the *shite*) appears to dance and sing, retelling its own story of days long past. There are only seven such pieces—'Rakuami, the Flute Playing Priest' (*Rakuami*), 'Yuzen, the Unskillful Umbrella Maker' (*Yûzen*; 28), 'The Octopus'(*Tako*), 'The Mountain Potato'(*Tokoro*), 'The Locust' (*Semi*), 'Backgammon' (*Sugoroku*), and 'Tsuen, the Tea Priest' (*Tsûen*: 27). 'Rakuami, the Flute Playing Priest' is particularly important as it dates back to before the middle ages, and 'Tsuen, the Tea Priest' is famous as a direct parody of the Noh play titled 'Yorimasa.'

98.   Young Woman (Oto) mask carved by Miho Irie

Kyogen Humor

Kyogen is an art of humor. But where does its humor come from? It is categorized as comedy, and while laughter is indeed an important element, it is not only the laughs that makes Kyogen of interest. Of course it is also true that there are many different elements that cause laughter. Therefore, let us have a look at the various aspects of Kyogen humor.

Felicitous Words and Peace and Harmony

In the section on Celebratory (*waki*) pieces we have already spoken about the large number of Kyogen that have felicitous words for their keynote. We mentioned that the Happiness God (*fukushin*) pieces have as their theme the bestowing of blessings. Also in Wealthy Man (*kahômono*) pieces such as 'An Umbrella Instead of a Fan' (*Suehiro-Gari*;93), though the auspiciousness of the theme itself (in this case the fan) and the bright happiness of the friendly relationship between Taro Kaja and his Master as they sing and dance together at the end, the piece is brought from the level of a simple story of Taro Kaja's failure, to a piece full of blessing and general good will. Most of the Farmer (*hyakushô*) pieces and Tradesman (*ichiba*) pieces also end with celebratory dances, songs or dialogue that indicate a harmonious end to the situation, stressing the felicitous nature of the piece as a whole. And this is true of pieces outside the Celebratory category as well. Pieces that end with laughter, such as 'Saved by a Resemblance' (*Jisenseki*) and 'The Demon-Faced Tile' (*Oni-Gawara*), are, in the final analysis, meant to be of a celebratory nature. The monkey dance in 'The Monkey Skin Quiver' (*Utsubo-Zaru*;80) produces a similar effect. While the Son-in-Law or Groom (*muko*) pieces generally take as their plot material some incident brought about by the stupidity of the son-in-law, the basic celebratory nature is clearly maintained in the auspicious nature of the custom of the First Ceremonial Visit itself and the felicitous dancing performed during the exchange of wine at the father-in-law's home.

Along with and closely related to the felicitous words and situations, we must also take care not to ignore the general element of ultimate peace and harmony inherent in the bulk of the repertoire. The dances in both 'An Umbrella Instead of a Fan' (*Suehiro-Gari*;93) and 'The Monkey Skin Quiver' (*Utsubo-Zaru*;80) produce this effect, as well as those in 'The Snail' (*Kagyû*; 37) and 'The Impudent Jizo Statue' (*Kanazu Jizó*; 24).

Drinking party scenes also produce a strong feeling of peace and harmony.

Wordplay

Since Kyogen is a comic form, it is only natural that part of its humor comes from the dialogue itself. Simple wordplay jokes that have no profound meaning are very much in evidence in Kyogen dialogue. One type of wordplay is a style of poetry called *shûku*.

The *shûku* style originated form the *waka* and *renga* styles of poetry, and is dependent upon a *double entendre* joke or pun for its humor. *Shûku* riddles are used in 'The Pilgrimage to Chikubu Island' (*Chikubu-shima Mairi*), 'Vinegar and Ginger' (*Su Hajikami*), 'The Fish Sermon' (*Uo-Zeppô* or *Uo-Zekkyô*), and many others.

Other types of *double entendre* and puns are used in such pieces as 'The Sound of Bells' (*Kane no Ne*;73) in which Taro Kaja mistakes the price of gold (*kane no ne*) for the sound of bells (also *kane no ne*) and 'The Half Delivered Gift' (*Kirokuda*;69+70) where Taro Kaja claims that 'six ox loads of wood' (*ki-rokuda*) is his own new name rather than the literal meaning. There are also the onomatopoeic parodies of chants and incantatious found in many of the Warrior Priest and Priest pieces and of foreign languages found in 'An International Marriage Problem' (*Chasanbai*), 'The Chinaman and his Devoted Son' (*Tôjin Kodakara*) and 'Chinese Sumo' (*Tôjin-Zumô*;89), and of animal talk in 'The Monkey Groom' (*Saru Muko*) and 'Fox Trapping' (*Tsuri-Gitsune*;3+4).

The highest form of Kyogen wordplay is found in the pieces that use the linked-verse poetry form called *renga*. Some examples are 'The Fuji Pine' (*Fuji Matsu*), 'A Debt Paid with a Poem' (*Hachiku Renga*), and 'The Winnow Basket Hat' (*Mi Kazuki*;58).

Here the battle of wits takes on a deeper meaning on both psychological and literary levels, rising far above simple wordplay and greatly enhancing the literary value of the pieces.

Human Comedy

Kyogen is full of characters who make outlandishly ridiculous claims and those who carry on in an extremely nonsensical and contradictory manner.

We spoke of these aspects briefly in the sections on Daimyo and Taro Kaja pieces. A close look from this point of view reveals Daimyo who are actually penniless but pretend to be wealthy in 'Wrestling by the Book' (*Fumi-Zumô* or *Fu-Zumô*), 'Nose-Pulling Sumo' (*Hana-Tori-Zumô*), 'Hired for a Riddle' (*Ima Mairi*), and 'A Man Poses as a Sword' (*Awataguchi*). Then there is the unlettered Daimyo with an impossibly poor memory in 'The Daimyo and the Bush Clover Blossom' (*Hagi Daimyô* ;83); the overly good-natured Daimyo who is nearly deceived by a crafty woman's tears until his somewhat craftier servant saves the day for him with a few drops of ink in 'Black Crocodile Tears' (*Sumi Nuri*); and the seemingly tyrannical Daimyo who ends up imitating and dancing with a monkey in 'The

Monkey Skin Quiver' (*Utsubo-Zaru*;80). It is interesting to note that a Kyogen Daimyo never becomes the object of social or political satire or criticism, but always manages to come off innocently light-hearted, unaffected, and universally lovable as 'just one of us.'

Taro Kaja in all his myriad manifestations depicts the very root character of the man-in-the-street. And he always comes off brilliantly delineated in sharp contrast to the other character or characters of any piece in which he appears. Taro Kaja as the great coward is seen in such plays as 'Sword Stealing' (*Tachi Ubai* or *Tachibai*) and 'The Brave Coward' (*Sora Ude*). Taro Kaja as the great lover of wine is seen in such pieces as 'Horizontal Singing' (*Ne Ongyoku*;79), 'Shedding the Demon Shell' (*Nuke-Gara*;41), and 'The Half Delivered Gift' (*Kirokuda*; 69+70). Taro Kaja-like characters who have these and other questionable but common human attributes are found in such plays as 'Akutaro Reforms' (*Akutaro*;20), 'The Stingy Aunt and Her Saké' (*Oba ga Sake*), 'The Stone God' (*Ishigami*;53), and 'A Bad Wife is Like a Bad Penny' (*Inabadô*).

Kyogen women are often introduced in the dialogue as 'a noisy (*wawashii*) woman.' They are all more stout of heart and sturdier of intellect than their husbands. In 'Unsuccessful Suicide with a Sickle' (*Kama-Bara*;29), she threatens her husband with his own pole until he agrees to go off to the mountain to work. In 'Cautious Bravery' (*Chigiri-Ki*;55) she vigorously encourages her cowardly husband to take revenge on his 'sometime' friends who have kicked and trampled on him. In 'Visiting Hanago' (*Hanago*;15) and 'Dontaro's Method for Handling Women' (*Dondarô* or *Dontarô*;59) she is quick to sense his unfaithfulness and chastise him for it. And in 'The Trial Rehearsal' (*Oko Sako* or *Uchizata*;56+57) she is the one who has been unfaithful, but she quickly covers for it by bluffing her husband literally out of his senses.

100

'A Demon in Love' (*Setsubun*;45) shows a demon, who is supposed to be strong, being humorously tricked and chased out by a member or the supposedly weaker sex.

We discussed earlier the frequent appearance in Kyogen of such characters as bandits, thieves, and shysters, but we also discover that each and every one of these 'bad guys' is amusingly good-hearted and foolish, similar to those who appear in the popular comic monologue art known as *Rakugo*. Then there are unexpectedly droll characters like the Arbiter in 'The Tea Box' (*Cha Tsubo*;13) who stops a quarrel between a Shyster and a Country Man by taking them both in.

Satire and Irony

There is a strong general tendency to dismiss Kyogen as merely a vivid reflection of the medieval social conditions in which the lower classes were beginning to seize power from the upper classes. However, as we have pointed out above, the bulk of those pieces dealing with masters and servants present no more than a simply humorous plot or an atmosphere of peace and harmony between the two classes, either of which seldom develops into any form of criticism or sharp irony. Still there are, of course, such pieces as 'Two Daimyos' (*Futari Daimyo*; 85+85), 'Lacquered-While-You-Wait' (*Nuritsuke*), and 'The Seaweed Seller' (*Kobu Uri*) in which the comparatively realistic presentation of disgraceful or cowardly behavior by a Daimyo is sharply ridiculed. In these examples, the level of satire is indeed quite high.

Among the Taro Kaja pieces, the overbearing egotism of a master is strongly hinted at and held up for ridicule by means of the dramatic device of a play-within-a-play in 'Shido Hogaku the Horse' (*Shidô Hôgaku*;62) and 'Sinner by Lottery' (*Kuji Zainin*;32), where Taro Kaja shows a lusty spirit of resistance. In 'Two to Deliver One Letter' (*Fumi Ninai*), Taro Kaja and

Jiro Kaja poke fun at their Master as they go on their way to deliver a letter to his homosexual lover. Their outlandish handling of the letter evokes healthy laughter.

Generally speaking, the Priest and Warrior Priest pieces present the richest satire of all Kyogen. The Priest in 'Sermon Without Donation' (*Fuse Nai Kyo*;21) is quite determined to get the regular donation from a Parishoner who has forgotten to present it to him for the first time. The Priest goes to great pains to remind the Parishoner subtly of his lapse of memory. Even so, when the Paishoner finally realizes why the Priest has returned so many times and offers the donation, the Priest tries to refuse to accept it. Here we see both greed and hypocrisy. The Priest in 'Priest Angerless Honesty' (*Hara Tatezu*) has just announced that his name is Angerless Honesty. When he is pestered by those he has been bragging to about his alleged calm and honest character, he does his best to hold back his anger, but it breaks through in the end – one more example of a hypocritical member of the clergy.

The Nenbutsu Priest and the Hokke Priest in 'A Religious Dispute' (*Shûron*;17) finally come to the realization that no matter what denominational adjectives one adds to his name, he is still the same Shakyamuni Buddha. This provides the means for the presentation of severe criticism of not only petty religious disputes but of all forms of narrow-minded sectionalism.

'The Shinto Priest and the Warrior Priest' (*Negi Yamabushi*; 35) and 'The Buddhist Sutra and the Shinto Dance' (*Daihannya*;15) show discord between mountain asceticism and Shintoism, and Buddhism and Shintoism respectively.

Lustful priests appear in 'The Mixed-up Acolyte' (*Hone Kawa*) and 'The Nun Nyakuichi's Revenge' (*Nyakuichi*). In the former, the old Priest is having an affair with the temple maid and in the latter he tries to seduce a nun. In both cases, the affair (or attempted affair) is revealed through the dialogue of a third party, which serves to further intensify the impression of sensuality for the viewer.

Among the large number of tradesmen who appear in Kyogen, the one who is held up for the sharpest ridicule for his crafty sales techniques is the Persimmon Seller in 'Hybrid Persimmons' (*Awase-Gaki*;9).

Surrealism and the Absurd

While their appearance is not as frequent as in the Noh, there are also many spirits of flora and fauna and other ghosts in Kyogen. All of the Dance Kyogen pieces have a ghost or spirit each. There are animals with supernatural powers in both 'Fox Trapping' (*Tsuri-Gitsune*;3+4) and 'The Badger's Belly Drum' (*Tanuki no Hara Tsuzumi*). Also, as we have seen earlier, there are a number of demons including Thunder himself, all of whom receive extremely humorous treatment. Among the plays of Kyogen, the bulk of which have everyday people as their heros, these types of characters do indeed fall into the surrealistic category. However, the group of plays that leaves the most intensely surrealistic impression as a whole is the Warrior Priest pieces, with their strikingly absurd plots. The appearance of the spirit of a giant crab deep in the mountains in 'The Warrior Priest and the Crab' (*Kani Yamabushi*;36) seems overly fanciful, but the possession of human beings by the spirit of an owl in 'The Hooting Warrior Priest' (*Fukurô* or *Fukurô Yamabushi*; 31) is unquestionably weird. This spirit possesses first the Younger Brother, then moves to the Older Brother, and finally seizes the Warrior Priest as well, and they all go off hooting merrily together. In 'The Snail' (*Kagyû*;37), at first only Taro Kaja is enchanted by the Warrior Priest's nonsense song, but finally his Master is also drawn into its magic and all three go off gayly chanting nonsensical words in a most joyful manner. The mesmerizing chant done by all three characters to end the play is similar in effect in these two pieces.

When the Kyogen piece titled 'Mushrooms' (*Kusabira*;38) was performed in the United States, the mushroom spirits with their flat round straw hats appearing through both the curtain (*agemaku*) and the low sliding door (*kirido-guchi*) gave American viewers the impression that the play was a parody of the Viet Nam war. They saw the Warrior Priest as America and the Mushrooms as the Viet Cong, something no Japanese had ever seen as a possible interpretation. But it is indeed true that the mushrooms, that keep multiplying no matter how hard the Warrior Priest prays, do indeed give the impression of a strangely virile and unconquerable life force.

Also the violence and outrage committed by the Passer-by upon the person of the Blind Man in 'The Moon-Viewing Blind Man' (*Tsukimi Zatô*;19) cannot be dismissed as simply an unjust act committed under the influence of alcohol. A 180° change of heart immediately after a warm rapport has been established is an overt expression of the basic ambivalent nature that lies hidden deep in the hearts of us all – the deep-rooted sense of the absurd that lies at the base of human personality.

The Joys and Sorrows of Life

'The Moon-Viewing Blind Man' (*Tsukimi Zatô*;19) is also a play rich in poetic sentiment with its natural background of the moonlit field on an autumn evening. This is one of the several Kyogen pieces that have few laughs and might best be called tragicomedy.

'The Blind Couple at Kiyomizu Temple' (*Kiyomizu Zatô*) is another Blind Man (*zatô*) piece that falls within the tragicomedy category. The fated meeting of a Blind Man and a

Blind Woman at Kiyomizu Temple is depicted here with tender pathos and delicate lyricism.

The Blind Man of 'Blindness, Sight, and Blindness Again' (*Kawakami*;46) is rewarded for his prayers with sight, but with the strict stipulation that he divorce his Wife as they are not well-matched. He is warned that if he does not abide by this condition, he will lose his sight once more. But his Wife adamantly refuses to even so much as discuss divorce. We see in this couple a confrontation between wordly gain and destiny, with the struggle for human happiness drawn in dazzlingly clear hues.

'The Water Throwing Son-in-Law' (*Mizu Kake Muko*;60) deals with the problem of water rights for irrigation, a serious matter in any farming village. This is brought to dramatic fruition through the subtle emotional balance inherent in such relationships as father and daughter, wife and husband, and son-in-law and father-in-law. "Just for this, I'll see that the two of you don't get invited to the festival, next year, and forever after!" This last line of the Father-in-law ends the play with a slightly bitter flavor reverbrating sharply through the humor of the situation.

The Woman (*onna*) pieces deal with trouble between man and wife. Aside from the humor of the henpecked husband, there is also a flavor of domestic warmth that runs strongly through them all.

In 'The Winnow Basket Hat' (*Mi Kazuki*;58) the Wife finally gets so disgusted with her husband's insatiable craze for *renga* poetry, which makes him ignore even the necessity to make a decent living, that she makes up her mind to leave him. Even so, it is an exchange of *renga* verses between the two that finally keeps them together. Here we see thoroughgoing connubial love expressed with depth and tenderness.

Also 'Fox Trapping' (*Tsuri-Gitsune*;3+4), the piece that is shrouded in secret techniques that are only passed down from teacher to student by word of mouth, we find the fear, the desolation, the pathos, and the desires that compete for priority in the heart of an animal presented as symbolic of basic human existence.

Kyogen Acting and Dramaturgy

Use of Time and Space

Kyogen is performed on the same stage as the Noh drama. It consists of a 24 foot (3 *gen*) square thrust stage, with a long narrow bridgelike passage way that leads off the up stage right corner of the main stage at an angle of about 100°. A thatched roof covers the main stage with posts at the four corners to support it. There is a similar roof over the bridgeway, and along the front of the bridgeway there are three small pine trees, known as the First Pine (counting from the one nearest the main stage), the Second Pine, and the Third Pine. At the far end of the bridgeway there is a Lift Curtain for entrances and exits and up stage left there is a low door, also used for entrances and exits.

This cubical space (so different from the modern procenium stage with its picture frame and front curtain) has given birth to unique styles of dramaturgy and acting techniques for Noh and Kyogen.

The dramaturgy and acting techniques of Kyogen, along with a bold combination of exaggeration and simplification, have brought about a perfect and brilliantly expressive form of theatre.

Almost all Kyogen pieces begin with an announcement of identity and purpose made by the character himself, called a *nanori*. This is generally carried out at the Name Announcing

Position (*nanori-za*, called the *jô-za* in Noh; up stage right), but there are also the *kata-nanori* which is executed on the Bridgeway behind the First Pine by such characters as Messengers and Shysters, and the *hon-nanori* which is executed down stage center by Daimyo and Wealthy Men. The acting technique for travelling from one place to another, called a *michiyuki*, also takes several different forms. The usual trip begins from the Name Announcing Position. The actor moves in an arc shaped path past the Sight Guide Pillar (*metsuke-bashira*; down stage right) to the Waki Pillar (*waki-bashira*; down stage left) where a turn is executed and he moves in a straight line back to where he started at the Name Announcing Position, resulting in a path that is shaped very much like an archer's bow. There is another type in which the actor does not stop at the Name Announcing Position on his return trip, but enters the Bridgeway and ends his trip at the First Pine. There is another in which he only proceeds a few steps down stage from the Name Announcing Position and then turns sharply left and goes up stage center to stop in front of the Small Hand Drum Position (*kotsuzumi-mae*). In all cases, this sequence of movement depicts a trip which could be from the master's house to the capital, to an uncle's house, or wherever the character may be going.

The triangular space up stage from a diagonal line drawn from the Shite Pillar (*shite-bashira*; up stage right) to the Waki Pillar (*waki-bashira*; down stage left) is consider to be *yin* space and is generally not used for acting. Thus the convention has developed that when a character is sitting on the floor facing front from any place in this area, he is not a part of the scene in progress. Two characters who are engaged in conversation with each other generally stand or sit facing each other, one at the Name Announcing Position (up stage right) and the other at the Waki Position (down stage left).

The passage of time and changes of scene are accomplished entirely by means of simple movement from place to place or with a single line of dialogue.

There are any number of Kyogen pieces that make interesting realistic dramaturgical use of the structure of the stage itself. In 'The Sound of Bells' (*Kane no Ne*;73) the four pillars of the stage are used to represent temples in Kamakura. In 'Unsuccessful Suicide with a Sickle' (*Kama-Bara*;29) the Waki Pillar is used as a tree where Taro ties his sickle and tries to run and throw himself against it to commit suicide (in the Izumi school script). In 'Piped In Sake' (*Hi no Sake*;71), the area near the First Pine on the Bridgeway is used to represent the rice storehouse and the middle of the main stage to represent the wine storehouse. A bamboo water pipe is passed across outside of the Shite Pillar to send saké flowing into the servant's mouth who is in the rice storehouse. In 'The Half Delivered Gift' (*Kirokuda*;69+70) the entire length of the Bridgeway and the width of the stage become a snowy mountain up which Taro Kaja drives a herd of 12 cattle in a most convincing manner with no more than a stick to aid him.

Dialogue and Gesture

The most impressive thing about the dialogue of Kyogen is the clear and well-projected voices of the actors. They are trained to open their mouths especially wide and to pronounce each syllable slowly and carefully. The voice is supported from the lower abdomen, and the shoulders and throat must remain totally relaxed, in order to give complete flexibility to the voice. Training stresses the minute control of the breath, both inhalation and exhalation, to produce the unique sound of Kyogen. However, if each syllable is simply pronounced slowly in a monotone, the words would not hold the interest of the audience for long. Thus a pattern of rhythm and nuance that brings to life the unique characteristics of the Japanese language, through its pitch, intonations and tempo modulations has been created over the centuries. There are slight differences between schools and individual performers, but the basic rule is to accent the second syllable of all meaningful words in a line of dialogue, raising the pitch with each accent, resulting in a stairlike progression, with the final word in the sentence brought back down to the original pitch or lower to end the sentence. This produces a perfectly balanced pattern of intonation. Tempo changes are added to the tone pattern to form a tapestry of highly expressive and pleasing sound.

In terms of elocution, Noh and Kyogen have points of both similarity and of dissimilarity. They share a simple formalized style of presentation. Also both are performed by male actors only, who neither use falsetto when they perform women's roles, nor change their voices perceptibly for characterization when performing any other roles. Further, the same types of characters appear in both Noh and Kyogen — women, lords, servants, priests and merchants.

The main way in which Kyogen differs from Noh is in its very candid expression of emotion. Amidst its formalized and high-toned dialogue, there are some extremely realistic emotional words and phrases. Noh has no dialogue or acting techniques like those of Kyogen for when a master shouts, "Hey, you rascal!" to scold his servant Taro Kaja, or when a woman stamps on the ground and screams, "Oh, how angry, how angry I am!" at her husband, or when people drink and sing and dance together and then laugh for joy at the end, or when a character is sad and weeps noisily.

The use of onomatopoeic words by means of which the performer produces all sound effects with his own voice is a technique that is entirely unique to Kyogen. When opening a heavy door, the actor vocalizes with *gara-gara-gara*; when using a saw, with *zuka-zuka-zuka*; when breaking through a bamboo fence, with *muri-muri-muri*; when pouring saké out of a full jug, with *dobu-dobu-dobu*; when pouring out the last few drops of saké from the same jug, with *pisho-pisho-pisho*; and when playing the *shamisen*, with *tsureten-tsureten-tere-tere-ten*. A good example of the particularly effective use of onomatopoeia in a Kyogen piece is the sounds used for the bells of Kamakura in 'The Sound of Bells' (*Kane no Ne*;73). Taking the Izumi school sounds for our illustration here, the bell of the Jufuku Temple is *jan-mon-mon* – just an average bell, the bell of the Enkaku Temple is *paaan* – a very thin bell, the bell of the Gokuraku Temple is *jaga-jaga-jaga* – a broken bell, and the bell of the Kenchô Temple is *kon-mon-mon* – by far the best bell of all.

On the other hand, the movement and gestures of Kyogen are basically the same as those of Noh. They both begin from the same basic pose known as *kamae* and the same basic style of walking known as *hakobi*. For the Basic Pose the hips are lowered slightly in order to shift the weight of the body down, resulting in a stronger sense of balance. If one begins walking while maintaining this pose, the feet naturally slide along the floor in the unique walk known as *suri-ashi*, familiar to anyone who has seen Noh and Kyogen performed. This peculiar walk is a technique that helps maintain the upper body in a strong, quiet posture, and is, therefore, not simply a meaningless decorative device.

There are variations of the Basic Pose and the Walk for different roles. Compared to the common pose and walk of Taro Kaja, Masters, and Farmers, that of Women and Old People is turned inward, giving a weaker impression, and that of Daimyo, Demons, and Warrior Priest is turned out, open and stronger, giving a braggadosio impression. While the feet usually slide along the ground as explained above, there is also the high-stepping walk of Demons and Warrior Priest, the halting walk of the aged, and special walking styles for non-human characters such as animals and ghosts. Other basic uses of the feet include the stamping known as *ashi-byôshi* and the simple rhythmical dance known as *uki-ashi* in which the knees are lifted one after the other and the hips are used like a spring.

If we compare Noh and Kyogen to the plastic arts, we find that this basic pose and way of walking are to these stage arts what sketching techniques are to the plastic arts. It is out of these two basic principles of movement that the various specific and concrete gestures are born and upon which they are firmly based. The term for expressive movements or movement sequences in Noh and Kyogen is *kata*, which can be translated as 'form' or 'pattern'. These movement sequences fall into several set types or classifications. For instance, joy or elation is expressed by means of a form known as *yûken* in which the open fan is waved twice in front of the chest, while weeping is shown by simply bringing one or both hands up in front of the eyes in a form called *shiori*. There are more than three hundred of these forms, some abstract and some concrete. These units of movement are woven together to form the tapestry of acting technique.

Kyogen and Noh have many of these forms in common, but there are also many that are unique to Kyogen. In fact, there are more than likely a far greater number in Kyogen. Because of the great number of everyday man-on-the-street characters in Kyogen who are involved in far more common human activities than in Noh, their means of expression is also natural-ly far more overt and diverse. Kyogen characters cry noisily, get drunk, and get angry, and they express these conditions in a most vivid manner. Within these expressive forms, there are any number of variations and nuances that are carefully delineated in training. However, there is a distinct difference between the expression of these human feelings and emotions in Kyogen and in, for instance, modern naturalistic stage realism. In Kyogen, each nuance of feeling is taught as a clearcut form, not improvised to suit the personal idiocyncrasies of the individual performer as in 'method' acting. But in performance, if the form is not instilled with energy and intensity, it comes off very flat and dull. The forms must be brought to life by the performer on the stage after he has learned and perfected them through long hours and years of strict and repetitive training. It is only in this way that a Kyogen actor masters his art and attains freedom of expression through the form.

Elements of Song and Dance

Noh is commonly spoken of as a theatre of music and dance, while Kyogen is generally thought to be made up of speech and conversation. This is indeed a most convenient explanation of their difference, if, that is, one is willing to accept a rather distorted view of the subject. However, when one comes into direct contact with the practical performing technique of Kyogen, one finds it impossible to accept such a simplistic view.

Zeami's statement that song and dance are the two basic elements of training has been the iron-bound rule for actor training in the world of Noh for ages past, and the young Kyogen performer is also given a solid grounding in the techniques of singing and dancing to effect thoroughgoing discipline and flexibility in the physical and vocal style of Kyogen acting. Even the most realistic of Kyogen gestures and vocal modulations derive directly from the strict discipline of the singing and dancing techniques. And song and dance themselves are also highly important techniques that are used directly in a large number of Kyogen pieces. A song is very often used as the theme of a piece or to stress a few important phrases or lines.

The voluptuous professions of love in 'A Demon in Love' (*Setsubun*;45), 'Drawing Water' (*Ocha no Mizu* or *Mizu Kumi*; 23) and 'Visiting Hanago' (*Hanago*;15) could easily fall into indecency and vulgarity were it not for the fact that they are enveloped in exquisite melodies and that they provide the prime moving force for the plot. And the songs that end both 'Blindness, Sight, and Blindness Again' (*Kawakami*;46) and 'A Religious Dispute' (*Shûron*;17) are natural extensions of the overall dramatic flow of the piece.

There are also a large group of songs in Kyogen that have no specific relationship to any particular play, called *komai-utai*, which are used as entertainment in the numerous drinking party scenes. As the name *komai* (literally 'small dance') *utai* (literally 'song') indicates, these songs are accompaniment for dances. (In contrast to the dances of Noh called *shimai*, these *komai* of Kyogen are indeed 'small' in terms of both weight of literary content and length). The Okura school has forty seven *komai* in its present repertoire and the Izumi school has seventy-one. Their music falls into three general classifications—1) those borrowed from Noh plays such as 'Kagekiyo,' and 'Yashima'; 2) uniquely Kyogen style songs such as 'Beneath the Willow' (*Yanagi no Shita*), 'The Rabbit' (*Usagi*), 'Lady of Reeds' (*Yoshi-no-Ha*), and 'Seven Year Old' (*Nanatsu-Go*); and 3) particularly elaborate and difficult pieces known as *Kyogen Ko-uta* such a 'Kamakura' and 'Sumiyoshi'.

There are several highly lyrical Kyogen pieces, such as 'Spring, Girls, and Saké' (*Wakana*;16) and 'The Plum Blossom Hut' (*Iori no Ume*;26), which are composed almost entirely of a harmonious combination of these songs and dances.

There are also a number of Kyogen pieces that use the

same four-piece orchestra as Noh — the flute (*nôkan*), the small hand drum (*kotsuzumi*), the large hand drum (*ôtsuzumi*) and the stick drum (*taiko*). This orchestra is used both in combination with singing and as purely instrumental accompaniment for dances. The plays that use the orchestra include the majority of the Celebratory (*waki*) pieces, and all of the Dance Kyogen (*mai kyôgen*) pieces, plus many others that require special effects or have some relationship to a sepcific festival or ceremony such as 'A Demon in Love' (*Setsubun*;45), 'Sinner by Lottery' (*Kuji Zainin*;32), and 'Chinese Sumo' (*Tôjin-Zumô*;89).

The actual number of Kyogen pieces among the 260 of the present repertoire that consist exclusively of dialogue is only eighty-six. And if those which have a stylized narrative tale (*katari*; a semi-sung-semi-spoken form that is often accompanied by dancelike movement) in them are excluded, only seventy-four remain that are made up purely of an exchange of spoken words. This means that more than seventy percent of the entire Kyogen repertoire has some elements of song and dance.

Masks, Properties, and Set Pieces

Kyogen is generally performed with the face bare of any decoration or covering, but there are about 50 plays in the repertoire with characters that are masked. Outside of the special god masks — the *koku-shiki-jô* worn by the Sanbaso in the ceremonial Noh play called 'Okina'; the *hana-hiki* used for the seldom performed Kyogen *furyû* pieces; and the *nobori-hige* and *tobi* used for *ai-kyôgen* roles in Noh plays of the God group — masks worn by characters in the regular Kyogen repertoire can be divided into three classifications; 1) those for gods and demons — Ebisu, Daikoku, Bishamon, Fuku no Kami, Buaku, Kaminari, and Hakuzosu—2) those for animals, plants, and their spirits – Monkey, Fox, Badger, Kentoku, and Usofuki – and 3) those for human beings – Ôji, Ama, Oto, Fukure, and Oryô.

Photo 101 is the God of Happiness (*Fuku no Kami*) mask used for the *shite* role in the play of the same title, and Photo 102 is the Daikoku mask which is used for the character of that name in 'Daikoku and the Poets' (*Daikoku Renga*), 'Ebisu and Daikoku' (*Ebisu Daikoku*) and 'The Shinto Priest and the Warrior Priest (*Negi Yamabushi*;36). These god masks have a human congeniality about them that makes them seem as though they truly are capable of granting worldly happiness. The Whistler (*usofuki*) mask, seen in three variations in Photos 103-105, is reminiscent of the comic *hyottoko* mask used in the *Kagura* dances and mimes of rural festivals throughout Japan. Its pursed lips do make it seem a bit starved, but a free and easygoing atmosphere also shines through. This mask is used for an extremely large variety of characters – the spirit of a mosquito, a scarecrow, an octopus, a locust, the spirit of pine resin, and the spirit of a mushroom.

The Buaku mask (107) and the Kentoku mask (106) also enjoy a wide variety of use. The Kentoku mask is used for such diverse animals as a cow, a horse, a dog, and a crab. The Buaku mask is used for all demon roles, thus appearing in all the plays of the Demon group, and it is also used as a property to frighten and threaten in 'A Demon for Better Working Conditions' (*Shimizu*), 'The Stingy Aunt and Her Saké' (*Oba ga Sake*), 'Shedding the Demon Shell' (*Nuke-Gara*;41), and 'Tea Chaff' (*Hikuzu*). Its glaring eyes, along with its big nose and mouth do seem strong and are frighteningly demonlike, but at the same time it is overflowing with charm and even sadness at its own timidity, making it a perfect symbol of the personality and character of all Kyogen demons.

The next most frequently used Kyogen mask is the Oto

mask (98+109). The conventional costume for a female role is a colorful kimono tied at the waist by a narrow sash and a long, narrow strip of white cloth that is wrapped around the head and allowed to hang down to below the waist from both sides of the head, and is known as a *binan bôshi* (literally 'handsome man hat'). Generally speaking, masks are not worn with this costume. However, when the character is particularly sweet and innocent, and not very beautiful, the Oto mask is used. Photo 110 shows a mask called *fukure* that is used for older, perpetually angry women. It is obviously simply a variation on the same basic theme.

The Ôji mask in Photo 111 is a rather exaggerated but clearly realistic old man's face. It is used for the *shite* roles in 'The Back-Straightening Prayer' (*Koshi Inori*), 'Three Grandsons Named' (*Saihô*), and 'Grandfather in Love' (*Makura Monogurui*). This mask seems to contain remnants of the coarseness of earlier forms of Kyogen. The Ama mask in Photo 112 is used for old nuns in such pieces as 'The Crying Nun' (*Naki Ama*;22).

The Monkey mask (118) is used for both 'The Monkey Skin Quiver' (*Utsubo-Zaru*;80) and 'The Monkey Groom' (*Saru Muko*;2). The Hakuzosu mask (113) is used for the *shite* in the first half of 'Fox Trapping' (*Tsuri-Gitsune*;3+4) when the fox is disguised as the Trapper's Uncle Hakuzosu, and the Fox mask (114) is used for the *shite* in the second half, when the Fox appears in his true form.

The properties used most frequently in Kyogen are various types of swords, conch shells (116), Buddhist prayer beads, and walking sticks. Next come such farm tools as shovels, hoes, and sickles, as well as saké barrels, gourds, chopping boards, butcher knives, and so forth, all of which give hints of the daily life of the common people of medieval times. The Shinto Kagura bells used by the Shrine Maiden and the Buddhist sutra scroll used by the Priest in Photo 115 are properties for 'The Buddhist Sutra and the Shinto Dance' (*Daihannya*).

However, the properties used symbolically for the greatest variety of articles and in the most amazingly effective manner are the fan and the cylindrical black lacquered box called a *kazura oke*. The fan is used 1) in all Kyogen dances, 2) folded, as all manner of whips, hammers, saws, knives, and such weapons as lances, halberds, bows, and swords, and even as a handmill in one play, and 3) opened, as boundary markers, wine pitchers, wine cups, doors, targets, and any number of other things. The fan is indeed the Kyogen actor's most versatile property. The *kazura oke* is used most commonly as a stool, and its lid as a large wine cup. But it also serves as a sugar container in 'The Delicious Fatal Poison' (*Busu*;68), as a tea box in 'The Tea Box' (*Cha Tsubo*;13), and as a persimmon tree in 'The Persimmon Thief' (*Kaki Yamabushi*).

The Japanese term for Set Piece is *tsukuri-mono* which literally means 'made thing' or 'construction,' as they are objects which are reconstructed, of wood and cloth, for each performance (as opposed to being permanent objects that are kept for long periods of time such as the properties described above). There are two categories of Set Pieces—1) those that stand on the stage and serve a similar purpose to that of scenery in a western style play, and 2) those that are carried by the performer like properties. Examples of those in category 1) are the blossoming cherry tree in 'Forbidden Blossoms' (*Hana Ori*) and 'The Flower Thief' (*Hana Nusubito*); the thatched hut in 'Bird Clappers' (*Naruko*); and the spider web in 'The Spider Thief' (*Kumo Nusubito*; 17) — all of which also appear in Noh. The *tsukuri-mono* of category 2) are easy to confuse with properties, but they are different in that they are constructed anew for each performance, as mentioned above. In 'The Race of the Horse and the Cow' (*Gyûba*; 118), a shock of black hair hung on a bamboo stick represents the cow and a shock of white hair hung on another bamboo stick represents the horse.

The scarecrow seen in Photo 122 is the creation of the Farmer in 'The Melon Thief' (*Uri Nusubito*; 12). It is made from three bamboo poles, a straw hat, a Whistler (*usofuki*) mask, a cloak called a *mizu-koromo*, and a length of rope.

Costume and Characterization

The terms used for the costumes of Noh and Kyogen is not the general Japanese word for costume, but the special word *shôzoku*. Noh costumes are highly stylized versions of the clothes worn by the nobility in medieval times, while those of Kyogen, while also quite stylized, are close to the type of clothes worn by the masses in those days.

Kyogen costumes are basically indicative of the type of character wearing them as opposed to being expressive of the individual character. A Daimyo wears a tall black hat (*eboshi*), a kimono with broad horizontal stripes (*dan-noshime*), over which he wears a cloak with broad sleeves (*suô*), and long trousers (*naga-bakama*) that drag on the floor behind him (16). A Master wears the same long trousers and horizontal striped kimono, but with a sleeveless cloak with stiff shoulders (*kataginu*) and no hat (86, 87+99). Taro Kaja wears a kimono of a plaid or checked pattern, short *hakama* and the same type of sleeveless stiff cloak as the Master but with a bolder, gaudier pattern (68). A Woman wears a bright patterned kimono tied with a narrow sash and a white cloth wrapped around her head and hanging down both sides (*binan-boshi*; 45). Priests, demons, and other characters are readily recognizable in their distnctive costumes.

Individual characters are created by the posture, movement patterns, and intonations of the performer. Kyogen is truly a performer's art, as he receives very little aid in exciting the imagination of the viewer from either his costume or his properties, and there are no lighting effects, scenery pieces, or makeup at all for him to rely on. Thus a highly developed technique with total control and concentration are necessary to bring to life the great beauty and depth of Kyogen.

Translator's Afterword

Kyogen has been the main reason for my residence in Japan and the center of my academic research and practical theatre work since the late 1950's. Its human universality and its great demands on the performer are the two aspects that have kept me totally fascinated all these years and promise to maintain their hold on my imagination for quite some time to come.

Detailed synopses of all the plays of the Kyogen repertoire can be found in my *A Guide to Kyogen* (Hinoki Shoten Publisher, Tokyo, 1968; revised 1980).

Don Kenny
Tokyo, 1982

99.
The Turret-like Scaffold (yagura) used as a property in 'The Fortified Beard' (Hige Yagura)

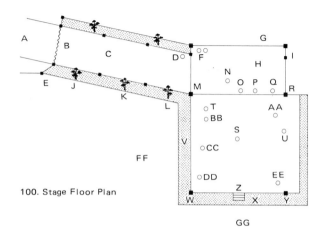

100. Stage Floor Plan

A — Green room or mirror room (kagami-no-ma)
B — Lift curtain (age-maku)   C — Bridgeway (hashi-gakari)
D — Kyogen position (kyôgen-za) E — Peek window (mono-mi mado)
F — Stage assistant position (kôken-za)
G — Pine or mirror board (kagami-ita)
H — Far up stage area or rear stage (ato-za)
I — Low sliding door (kirido-guchi)
J — Third pine (san-no-matsu)   K — Second pine (ni-no-matsu)
L — First pine (ichi-no-matsu)   M — Stick drum position (taiko-za)
N — Large hand drum position (ôtsuzumi-za)
O — Front of large and small hand drums (taishô-mae)
P — Small hand drum position (kotsuzumi-za)
Q — Flute position (fue-za)   R — Flute pillar (fue-bashira)
S — Stage center (shô-chû)   T — Usual position (jô-za)
U — Chorus position (jiutai-za) V — White pebbles (shirasu)
W — Sight guide pillar (metsuke-bashira)
X — Stair (shirasu-hashigo)   Y — Waki pillar (waki-bashira)
Z — Down stage center (shôsaki) AA — Up stage left (ji-mae)
BB — Name announcing position (nanori-za)
CC — Center stage right (waki-shô)
DD — Down stage right corner (sumi)
EE — Waki position (waki-za)
FF — Side seats (waki shômen)   GG — Front seats (shômen)

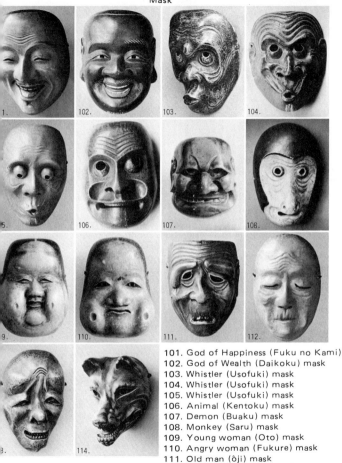

101. God of Happiness (Fuku no Kami)
102. God of Wealth (Daikoku) mask
103. Whistler (Usofuki) mask
104. Whistler (Usofuki) mask
105. Whistler (Usofuki) mask
106. Animal (Kentoku) mask
107. Demon (Buaku) mask
108. Monkey (Saru) mask
109. Young woman (Oto) mask
110. Angry woman (Fukure) mask
111. Old man (òji) mask
112. Old woman (Ama) mask
113. Priest Hakuzôsu mask
114. Fox (Kitsune) mask

121

115. Shinto Kagura dance bells and Buddhist sutra scroll
116. Conch shell carried by Warrior Priests (Yamabushi)

117. Spider's web

122

118. Cow and Horse

119. Seirai's Hawk

120. Wine shop sign

123

121. Portable tea shop

122. Scarecrow

123. Seven tools

124

HOIKUSHA COLOR BOOKS

ENGLISH EDITIONS

Book Size 4″×6″

COLORED ILLUSTRATIONS FOR NATURALISTS

Text in Japanese, with index in Latin or English.

Book Size 6″ × 8″

< ENGLISH EDITIONS >

SHELLS
OF
THE
WESTERN
PACIFIC
IN
COLOR

Book Size 7″×10″

〈vol. I〉by Tetsuaki Kira
(304 pages, 72 in color)
〈vol. II〉by Tadashige Habe
(304 pages, 66 in color)

FISHES
OF
JAPAN
IN
COLOR

Book Size 7″×10″

by Toshiji Kamohara
(210 pages, 64 in color)